LA STORIA DEI NUMERI

THE NUMBER STORY

SMALL BOOK ONE

ENGLISH - ITALIAN

Numbers Teach Children
Their Number Names

written and illustrated by

MISS ANNA

Early Reader Edition of *The Number Story 1*
Bronze Medal Winner, 2016 Wishing Shelf Book Award

Library of Congress Control Number: 2018902040

Names: Miss Anna, author.
Title: Number story : numbers teach children their number names / Miss Anna.
Description: Portland, OR: Lumpy Publishing, 2018.
Identifiers: ISBN 978-1-945977-15-2 | LCCN 2018902040
Summary: The pictures and rhymes present stories which introduce numbers 0-10.
Subjects: LCSH Numeration—English--Italian--Pictorial works--Juvenile literature. | BISAC JUVENILE NONFICTION /
Languages: English--Italian
Classification: LCC QA141.3 .M57 2018 | DDC 513—dc23

Publisher: Lumpy Publishing
Website: www.missannabooks.com
Email: missanna@missannabooks.com

Paperback: ISBN 978-1-945977-15-2
Printed in the U.S.A.   1 3 5 7 9 10 8 6 4 2

Volete imparare
i nomi dei numeri?

It is very easy and a lot of fun!

E' molto semplice e divertente!

Say-along our little jingle

Cantiamo insieme il ritornello.

starting from Number One!

Iniziamo dal Numero Uno!

1
ONE looks like my one finger.
UNO
è come il mio ditino.

ONE!
UNO!

2

TWO trails a tail.

DUE

ha una codina.

UNA CODINA!

3

THREE has bumps.

TRE

è cicciottello.

CICCIOTTELLO!

4

FOUR carries a sail.

QUATTRO

ha una vela.

4
A SAIL!
UNA VELA!

5

FIVE   is a racing track.

CINQUE

è una pista da corsa.

VROOM
VROOM!

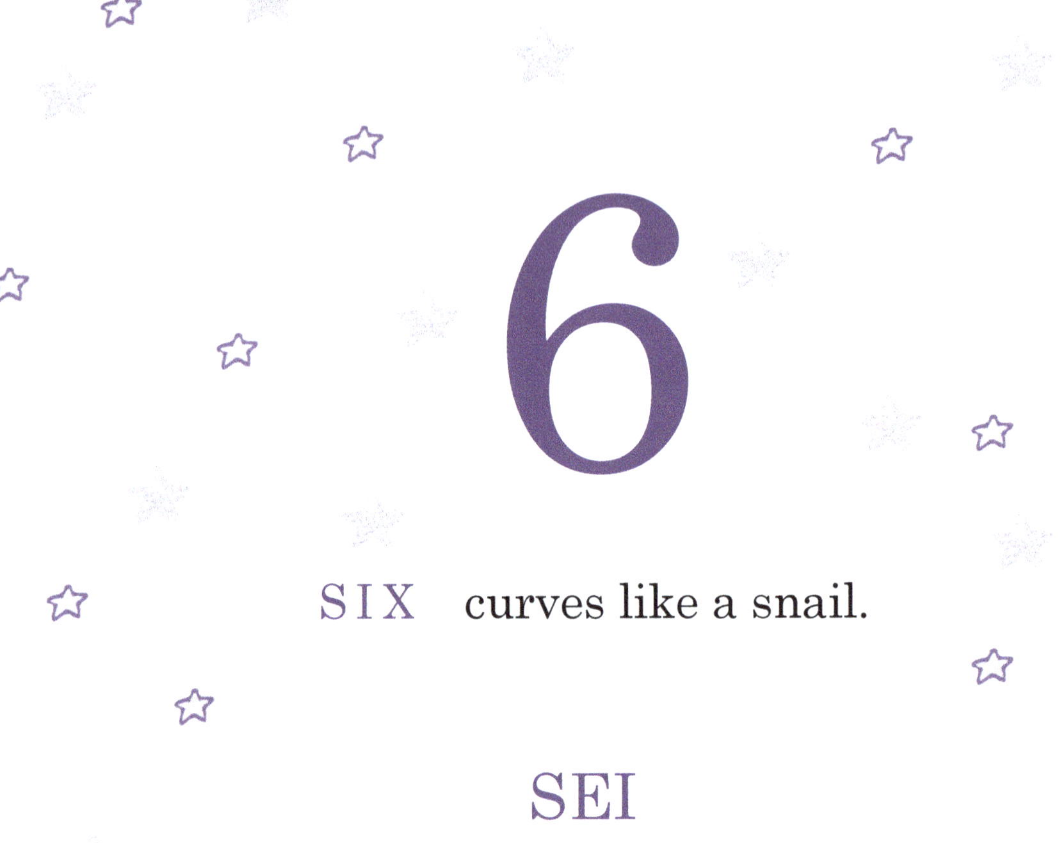

6

SIX   curves like a snail.

SEI

è una lumachina.

A SNAIL!

UNA LUMACHINA!

7

SEVEN has a sharp angle.

SETTE

ha un angoletto.

OUCH!
ATTENTO!

EIGHT is rollercoaster rails.

OTTO

è una montagne russa.

YIPPIEEE!
YIPPEE!

NINE is a bubble on a stick.

NOVE

é una bolla su un bastone.

A BUBBLE! UNA BOLLA!

10

TEN   is an eye of a whale.

DIECI

è un occhiodi una balena.

Ved il mio occhiolino?

And
E

0

ZERO   is an empty pail.

ZERO

è un secchio vuoto.

IT'S
EMPTY!
É VUOTO!

Thank you for playing with us today.

We had a lot of fun too!

Grazie per aver giocato con noi oggi.

Anche noi ci siamo divertiti molto!

We are your Number friends,
Zero to Ten,
Who will be here for you~
Noi siamo i tuoi amici Numeri,
da Zero a Dieci,
e saremo qui per te~

Bye-bye now!
See you again soon.
Ciao ciao!
Ci rivediamo presto!

The Numbers are *SINGING* too!

To sing-a-long, look for Miss Anna Number Story
at your favorite music store like iTUNES.

MP3

Numbers 0-10
IDENTIFYING
& COUNTING

Numbers 11-20
& Ordinals
first, second, third...

Numbers 0-100
& Place Values
ones, tens, hundreds...

About Clocks
& Telling Time
hours, minutes, second...

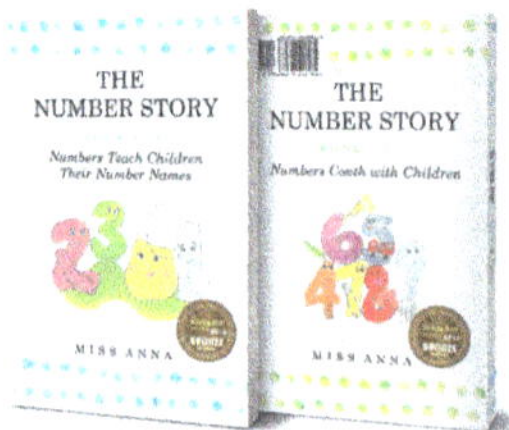

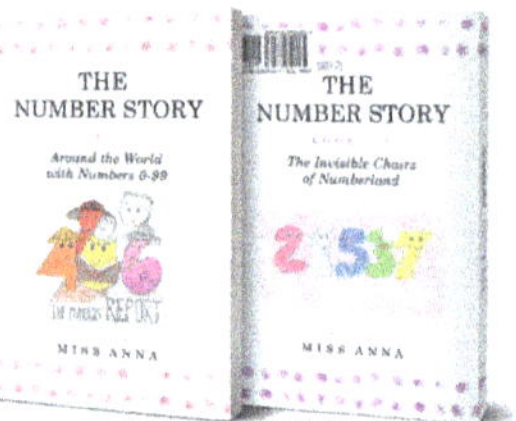

Number Story 1 & 2
isbn: 978-0-996216-48-7

Number Story 3 & 4
isbn: 978-1-945977-01-5

Number Story 5 & 6
isbn: 978-1-945977-06-0

Number Story 7 & 8
isbn: 978-1-949320-40-

For more Miss Anna books to love,
visit us at

www.missannabooks.com

Numbers are working hard all over the world!
Come Travel the World with Us!

www.ingramcontent.com/pod-product-compliance
Lightning Source LLC
Chambersburg PA
CBHW041101050726
47599CB00018B/2222